Pablo Helguera

Suite Panamericana

Jorge Pinto Books Inc.
New York

Suite Panamericana
By Pablo Helguera

© Text and Illustrations, Copyright 2011 by Pablo Helguera

All rights reserved. This book may not be reproduced in whole or in part, in any form (beyond copying permitted by Sections 107 and 108 of the United States Copyright Law, and except limited excerpts by reviewer for the public press), without written permission from Jorge Pinto Books Inc. 151 East 58th Street, New York, NY 10022.

Published by Jorge Pinto Books Inc., website: www.pintobooks.com

Book design by Charles King, website: www.ckmm.com

Cover Illustration and design: © Pablo Helguera

ISBN13: 978-1-934978-54-2
ISBN10: 1-934978-54-X

The 200 collage works in *Suite Panamericana* conform part of the art project *The School of Panamerican Unrest*, a trans-continental trip by ground made in the summer of 2006. As part of this project, I drove 25,000 miles from Anchorage, Alaska, to Tierra del Fuego, Chile, carrying a collapsible 20 × 20 × 15ft structure in the form of a schoolhouse stopping at 27 cities in the Americas and presenting performances, civic actions and public discussions along the way. The School of Panamerican Unrest project, initiated in 2003, seeks to establish connections between the different communities in the Americas and investigate the remnants of the XIXth century's ideals of inter-continental integration at a cultural level.

Upon my return from the 4-month ground journey, I came back facing a challenging process of physical and mental recovery from this experience. I had maintained a daily blog which relayed the main facts and events. Yet, the experiences and reflections of the trip had been far more complex than what could possibly be reported through that online blog, and upon my return I felt overwhelmed by the daunting task of tackling that narration. As a result, I instinctively took to making small collages, trying to find adequate images and words from old books and educational publications that would directly or metaphorically reference specific experiences and thoughts related to that journey. In this sense, the *Suite Panamericana* became a sort of counter-narrative to the literal narrative of the journey, a subconscious complement to the spelled-out descriptions of the customs crossings, the political and social events unfolding around the project, and the personal interactions that took place along the way. In a very personal way, I regard this series as operating with the internal logic similar to a dream sequence with fragmentary, if recurring, questions, affirmations, and obsessions, in-keeping with the simultaneously inquisitive and experiential components of the project.

Pablo Helguera

AN ACCIDENT: AMERICA

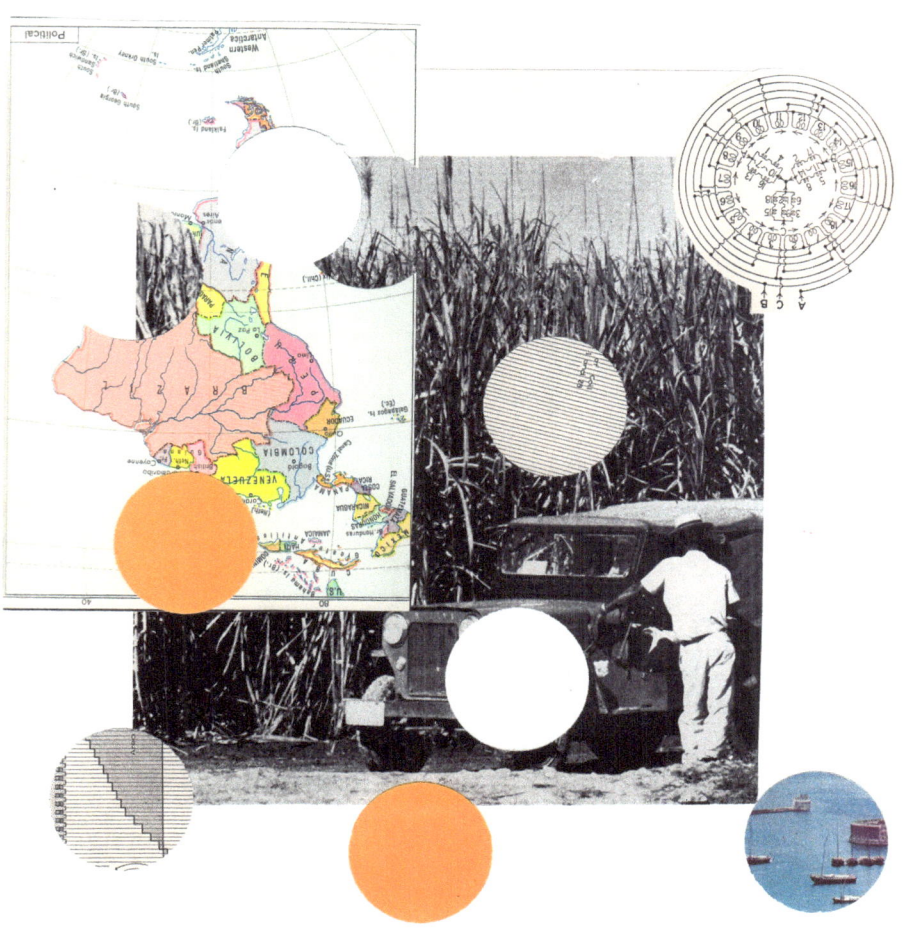

The more believable image is that of the chaotic singularity, where the breakdown of law leads to complete randomness, so that the emerging material and influences have no in-built organization at all.

A HUNDRED YEARS AGO

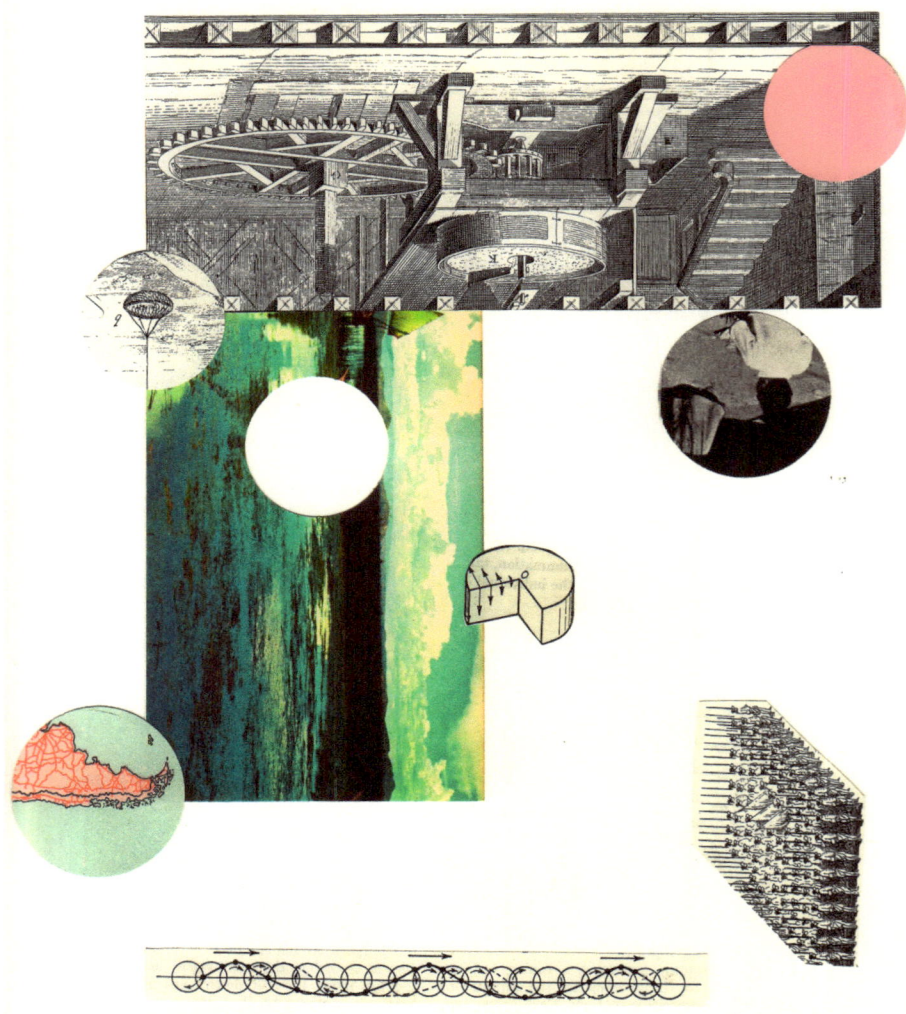

That is the way the matter stands today.

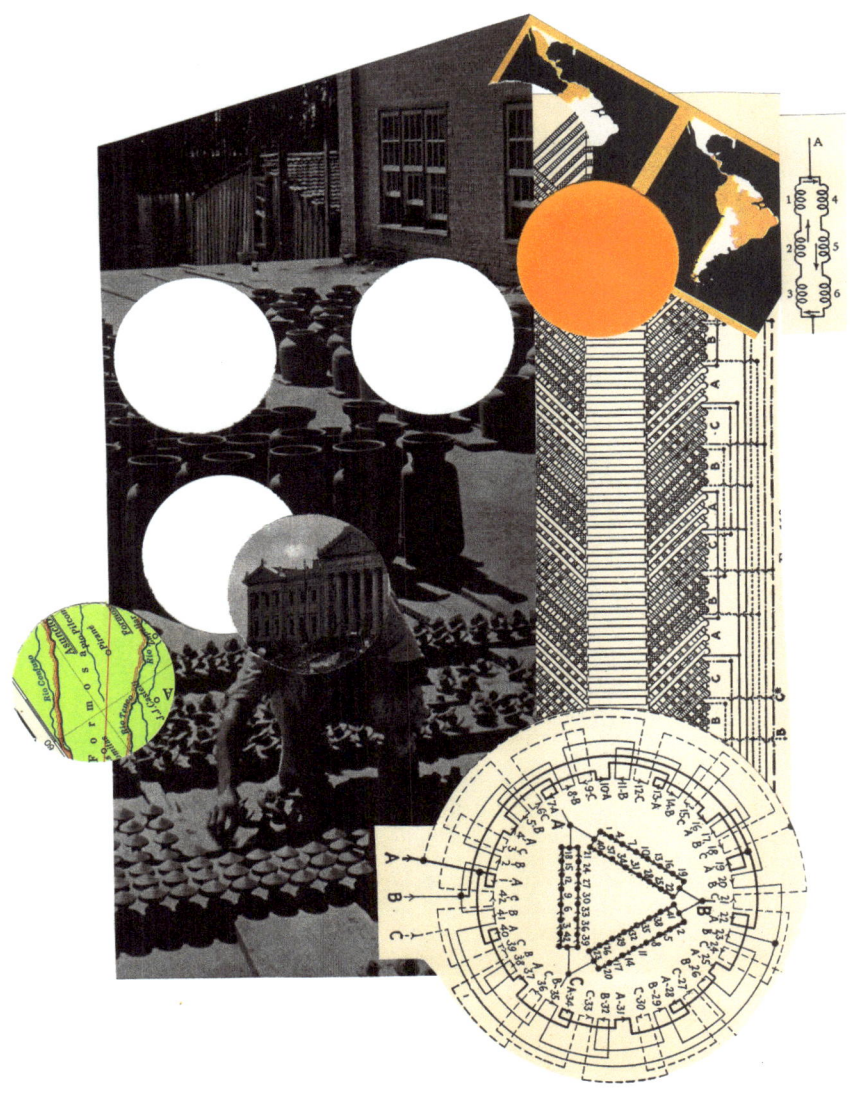

MAN IN HIS RELATION TO OTHERS

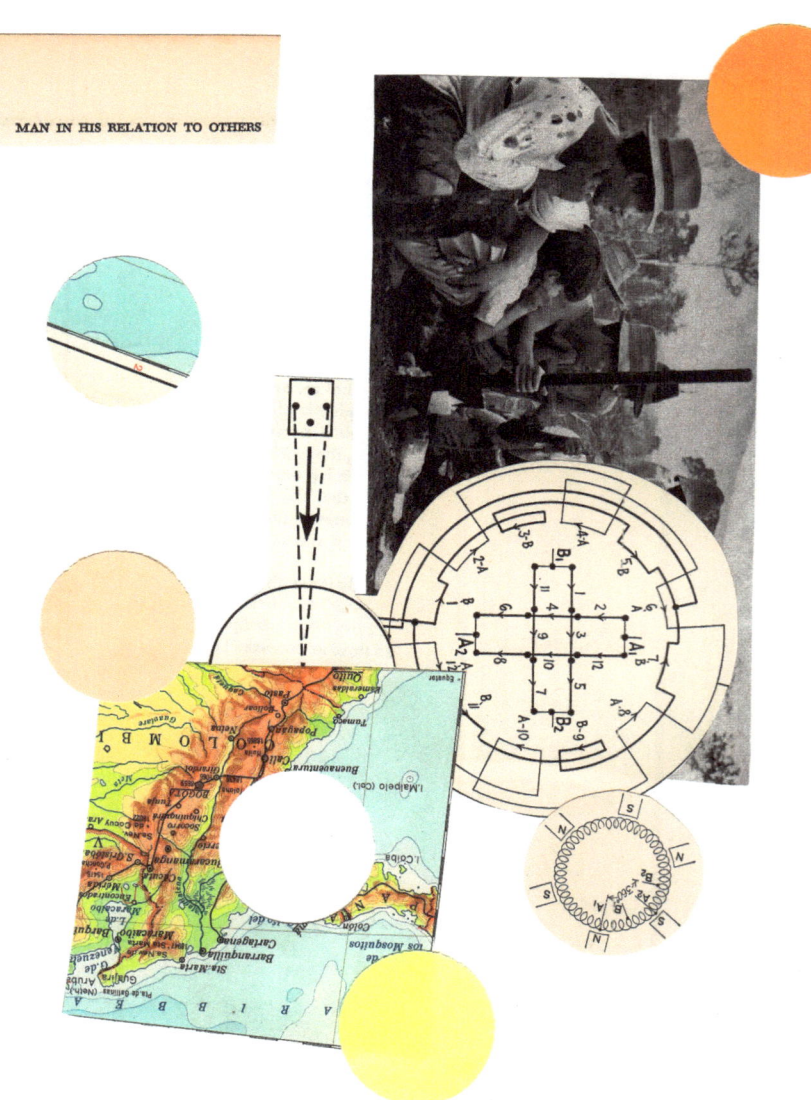

An ancient Chinese adept has said: But if the wrong man uses the right means, the right means work in the wrong way.

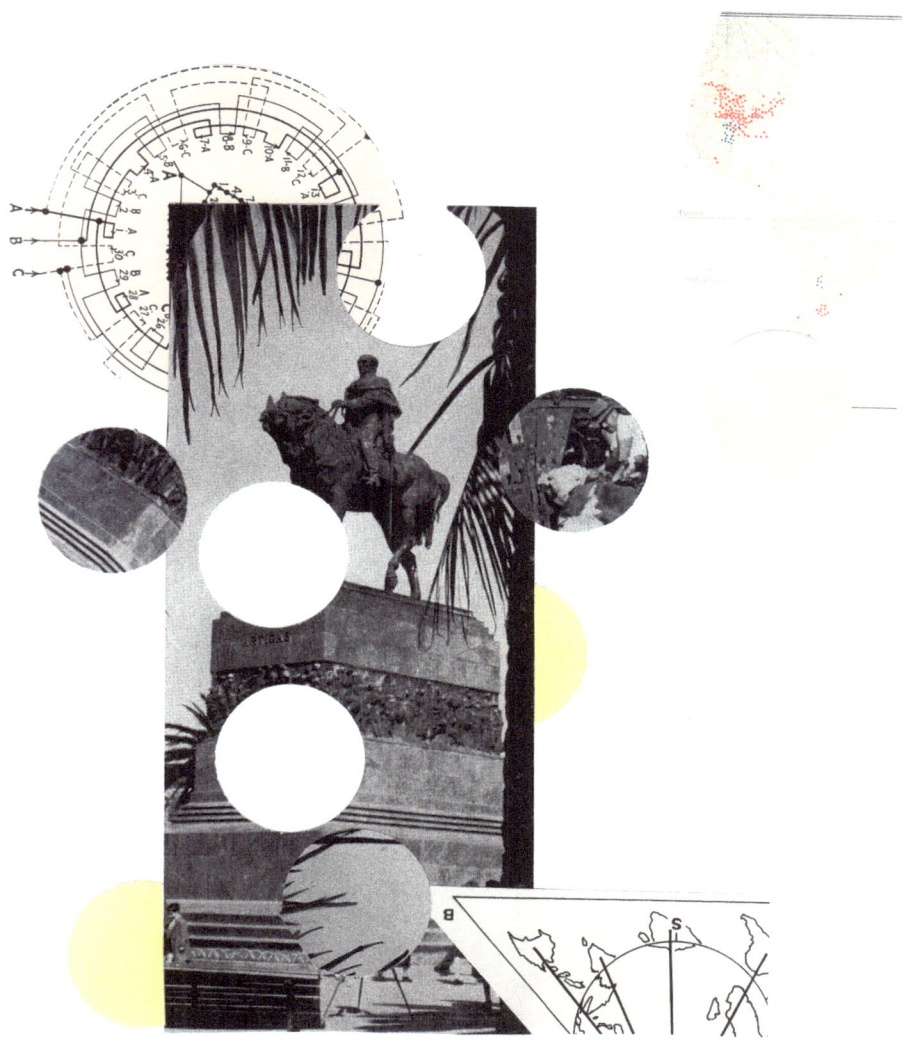

But in this they are certainly mistaken. '

Facing the unknowable

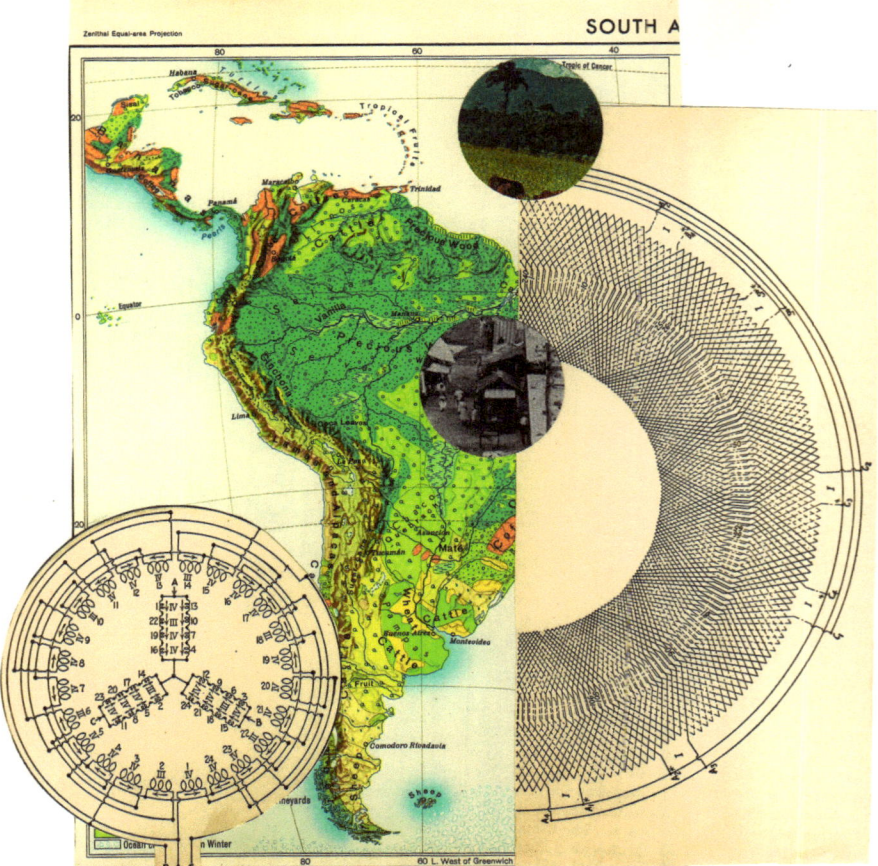

Although at present only a fragment of the total picture is understood, it is easy to suppose that, in principle at least, everything that ever happens in the universe is completely determined by everything else.

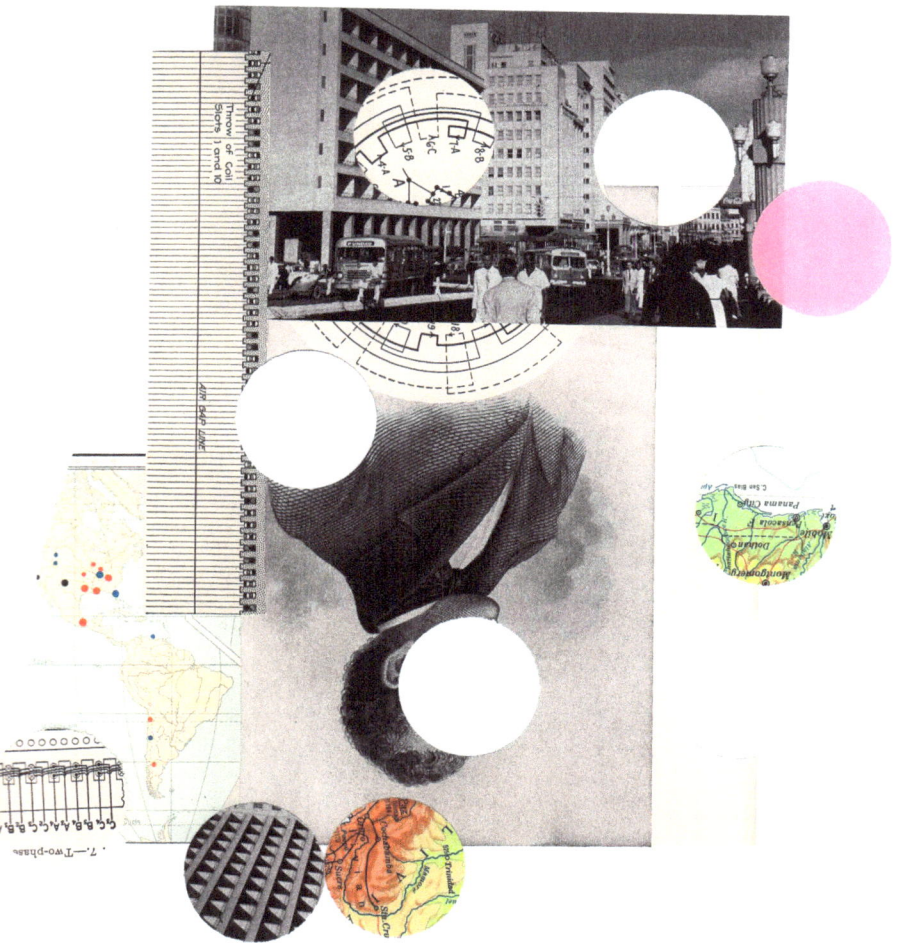

THE FLAG OF OUR UNION FOREVER.

In a new age old terms do indeed acquire new meanings. But the process is very gradual; and

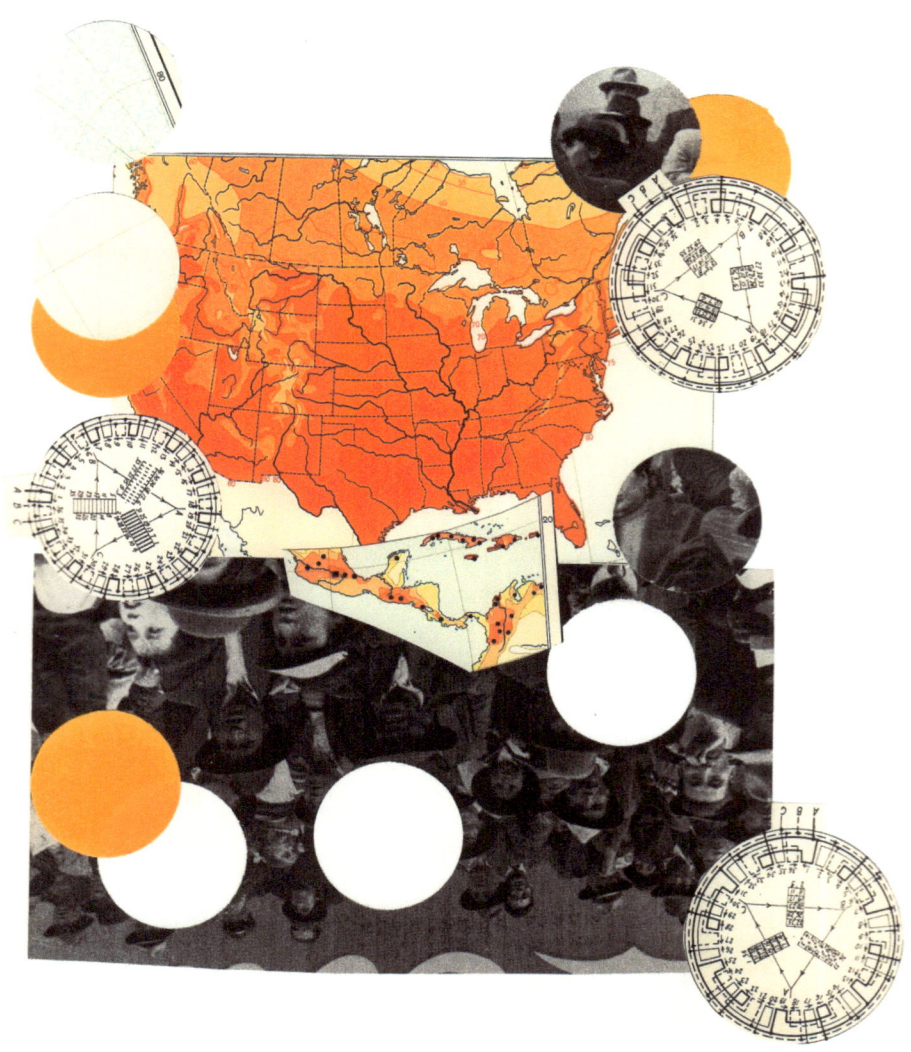

This conundrum recalls a more familiar problem of geometry concerned with geographical projections.

THE PRIMORDIAL IMAGES

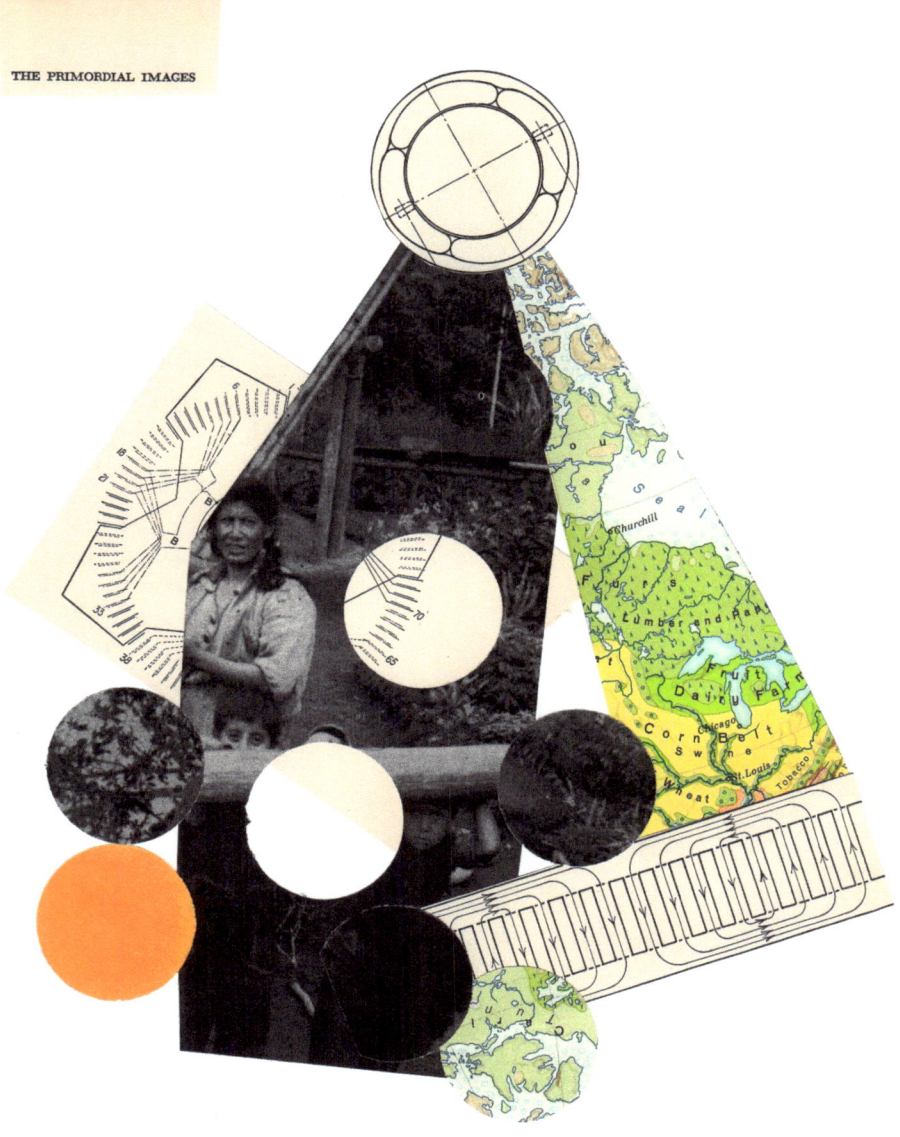

out in light a-cross our way, And ev-'ry hill and vale a-far Was gladden'd by its ray.
faint and wea-ry with de-lay. Ah, me! how earnest-ly I long To thee to fly a-way!
stranger's smile give joy to me; Oh! for some sea-bird's buoyant wing To bear me home to thee!

THE SONG OF THE IMMIGRANT

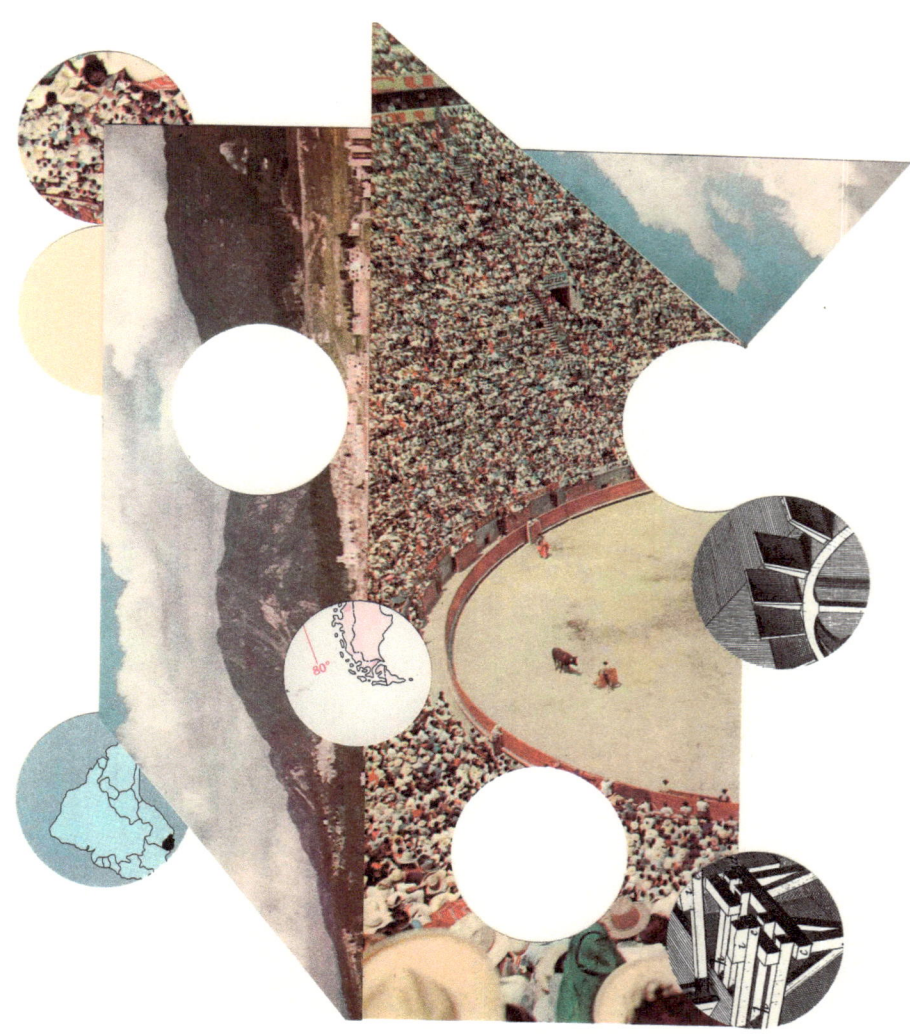

This sounded like foolishness, and for a long time it was so regarded. But it was mostly truth.

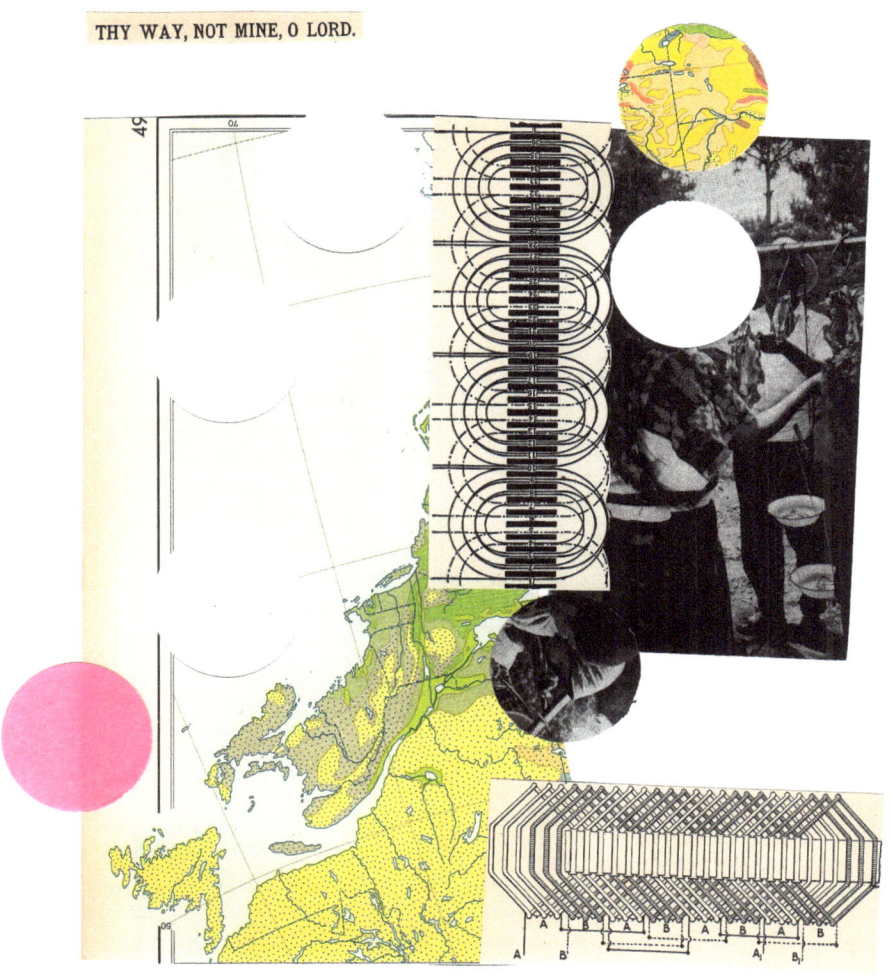

WHAT THE INDIVIDUAL DOES

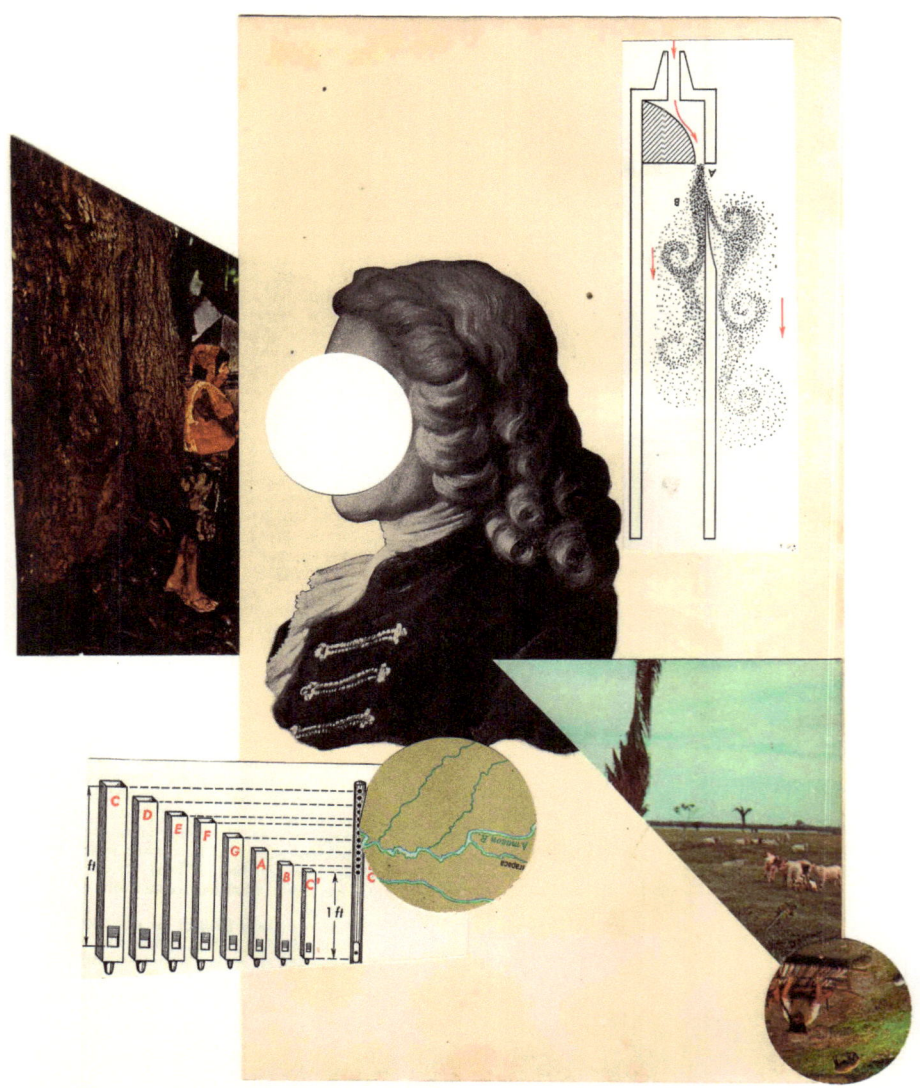

This ideal final arrangement never takes place

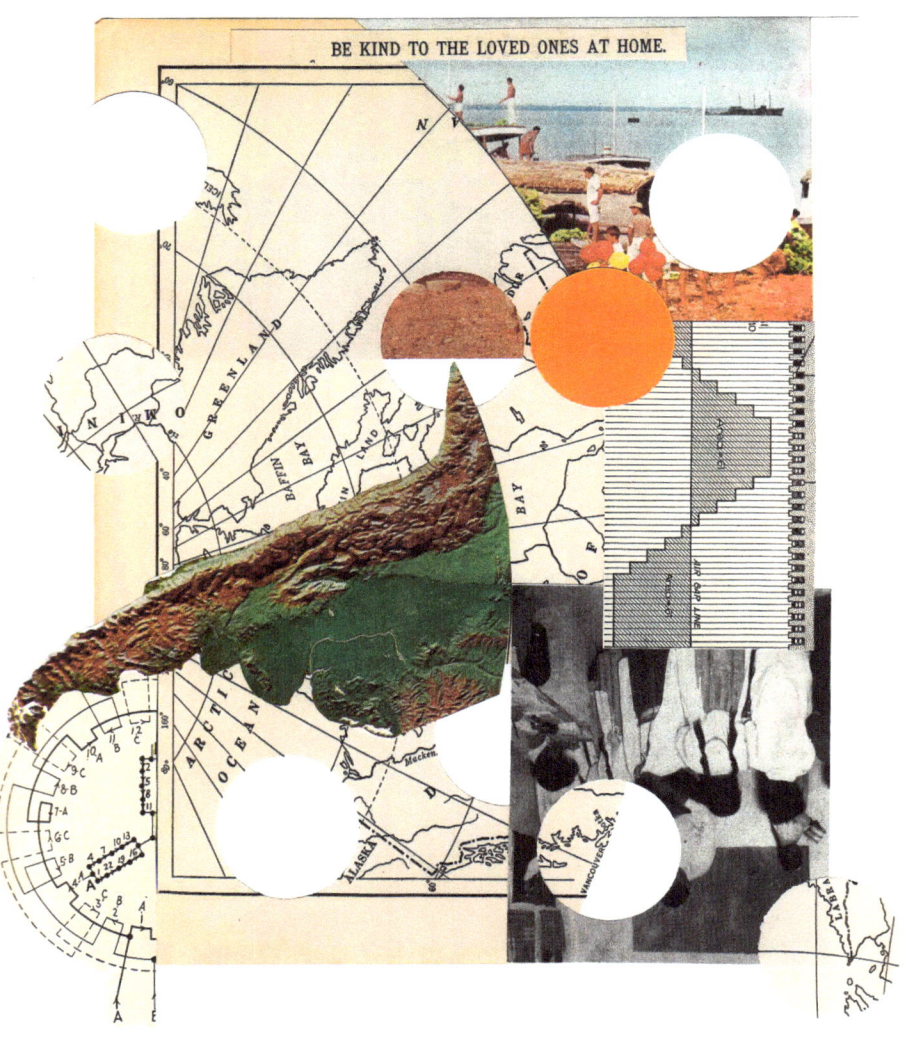

in the Rainy Tropics

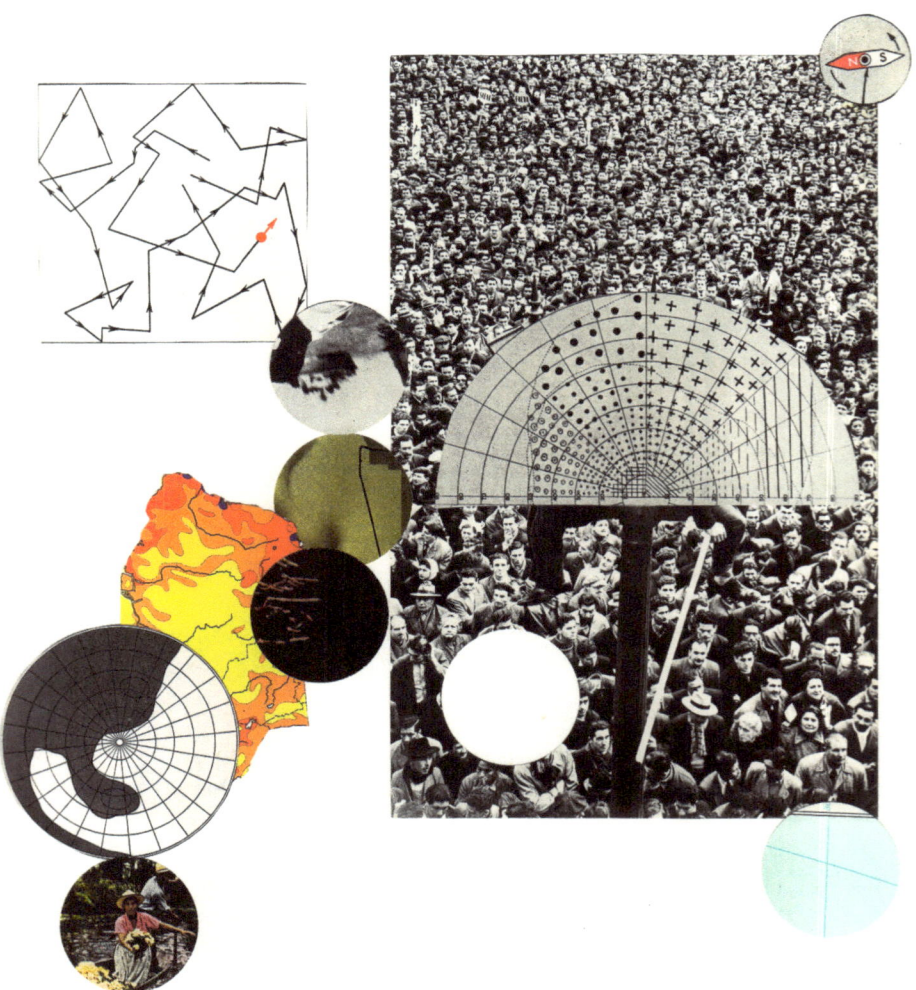

They have lost their eyes trying to get used to their new environment, but they have not given up.

spoken (simply)

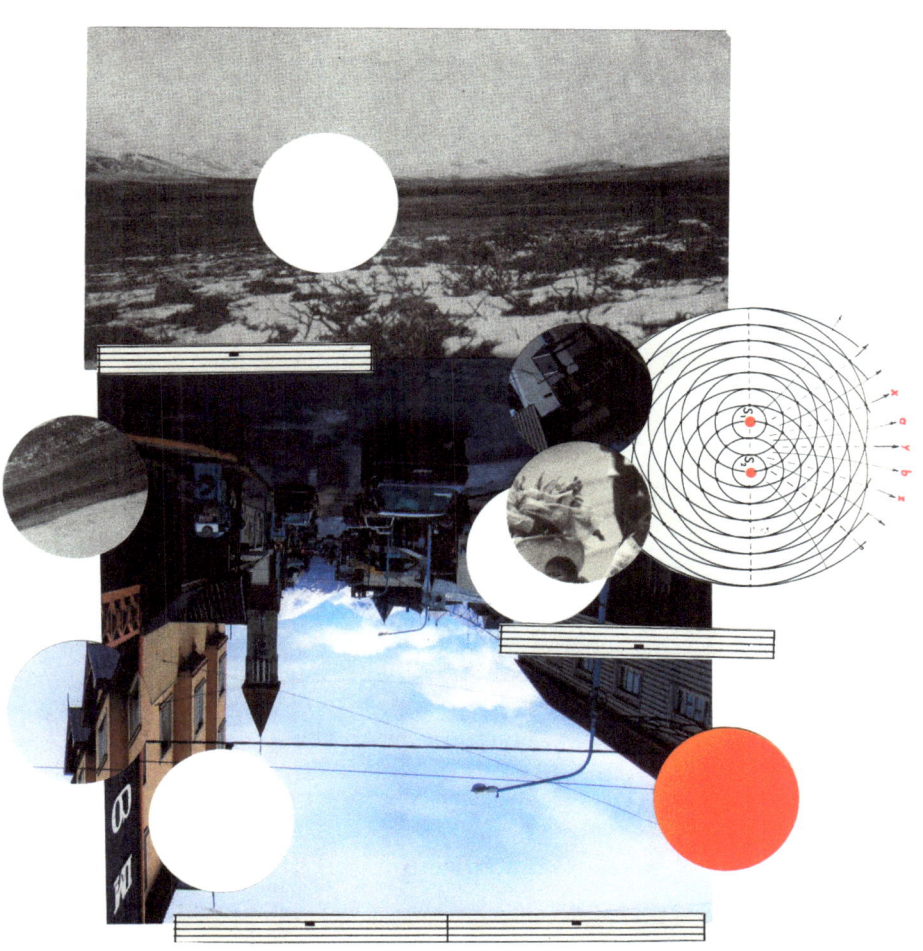

But no one had ever told him why
this happened.

SWING LOW, SWEET CHARIOT.

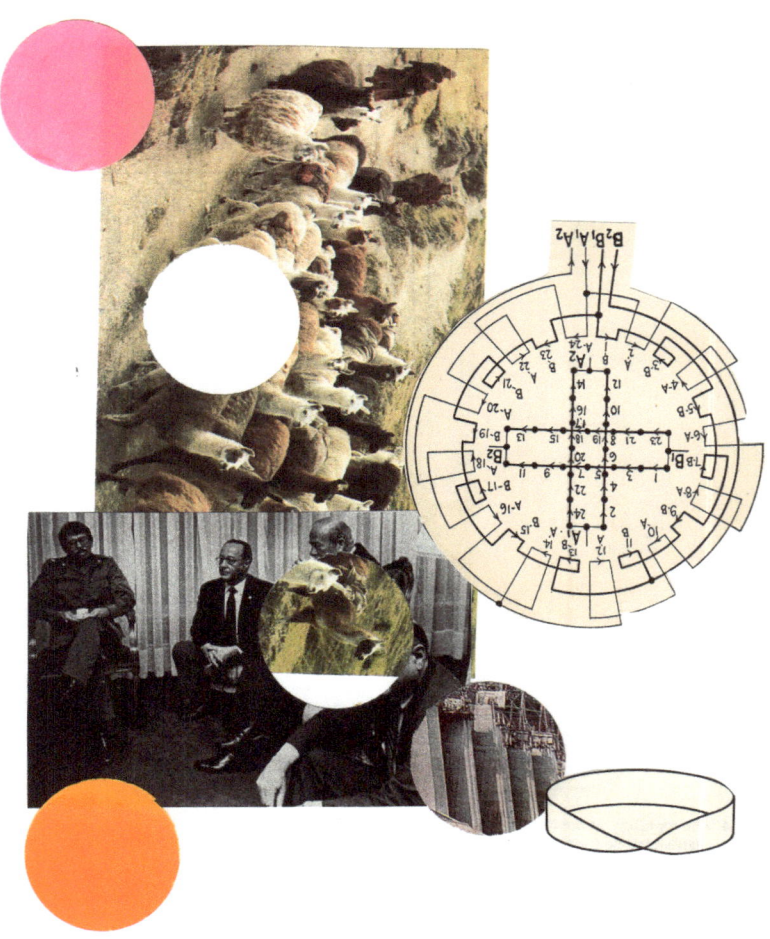

Individuals in society, and above all in the State, may control the stream of life to a certain extent and regulate it like a canal.

IT IS BETTER TO LAUGH THAN BE SIGHING.

When it occurs to a man that nature does not regard him as important, and that she feels she would not maim the universe by disposing of him, he at first wishes to throw bricks at the temple, and he hates deeply the fact that there are no bricks and no temples.

A MILLION LITTLE DIAMONDS

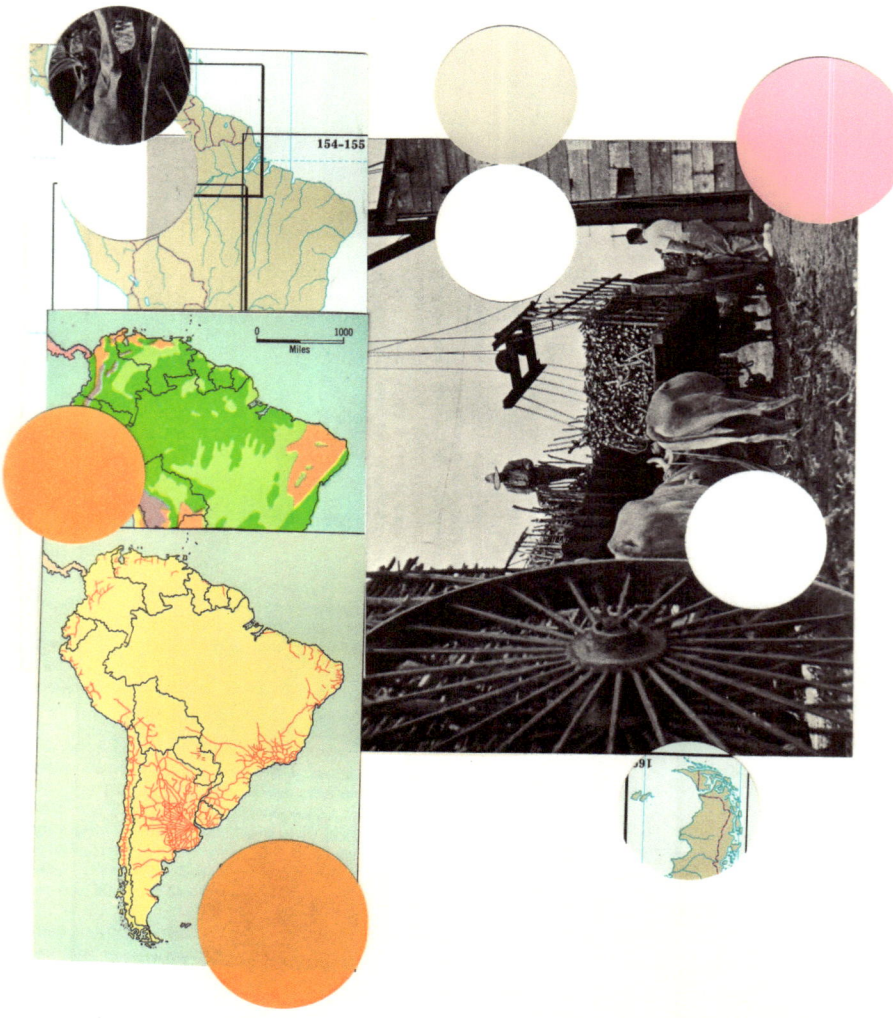

Each one of us constructs the world in his own way, whether as actor or observer, and we have no means of determining the success of translations from one frame of reference to another.

On mental maps

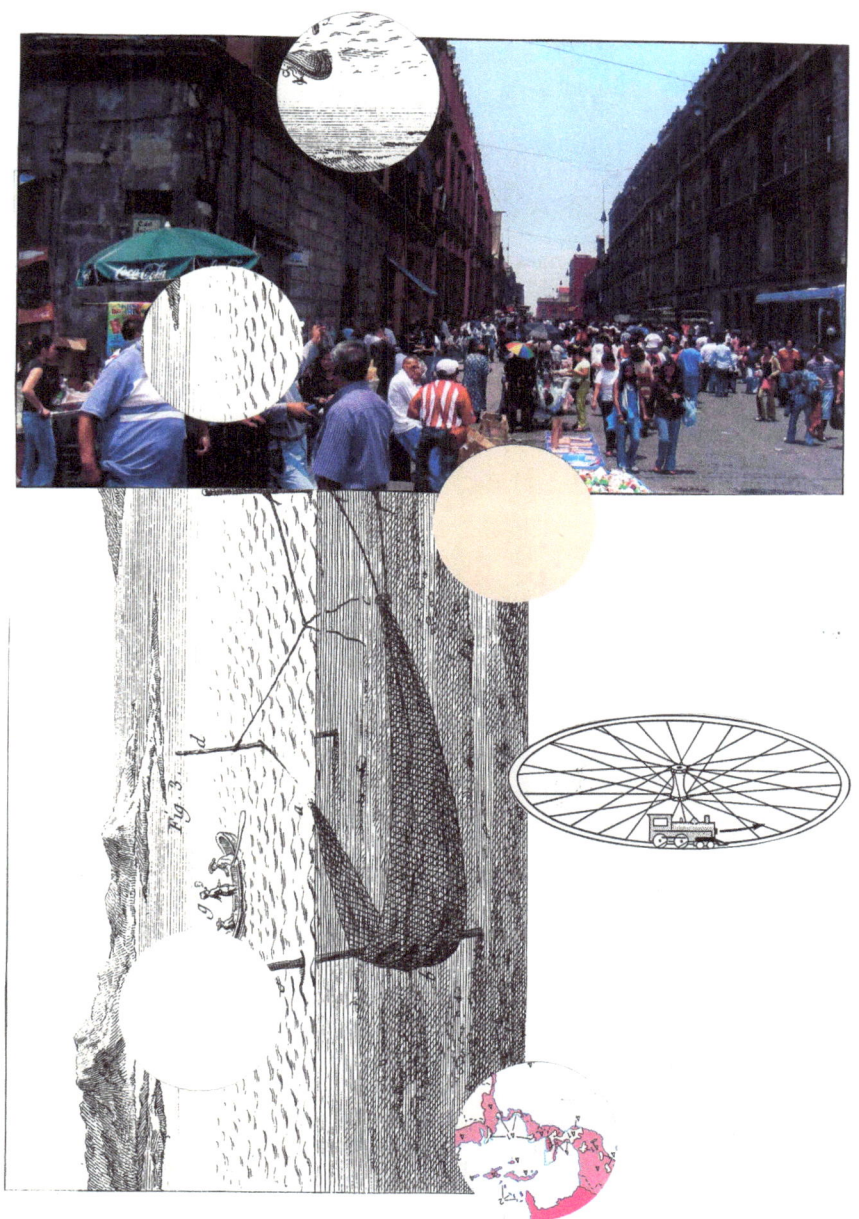

If one wanted to let his imagination loose, here would be the chance.

BLEST SYMBOL OF BLEST NAME.

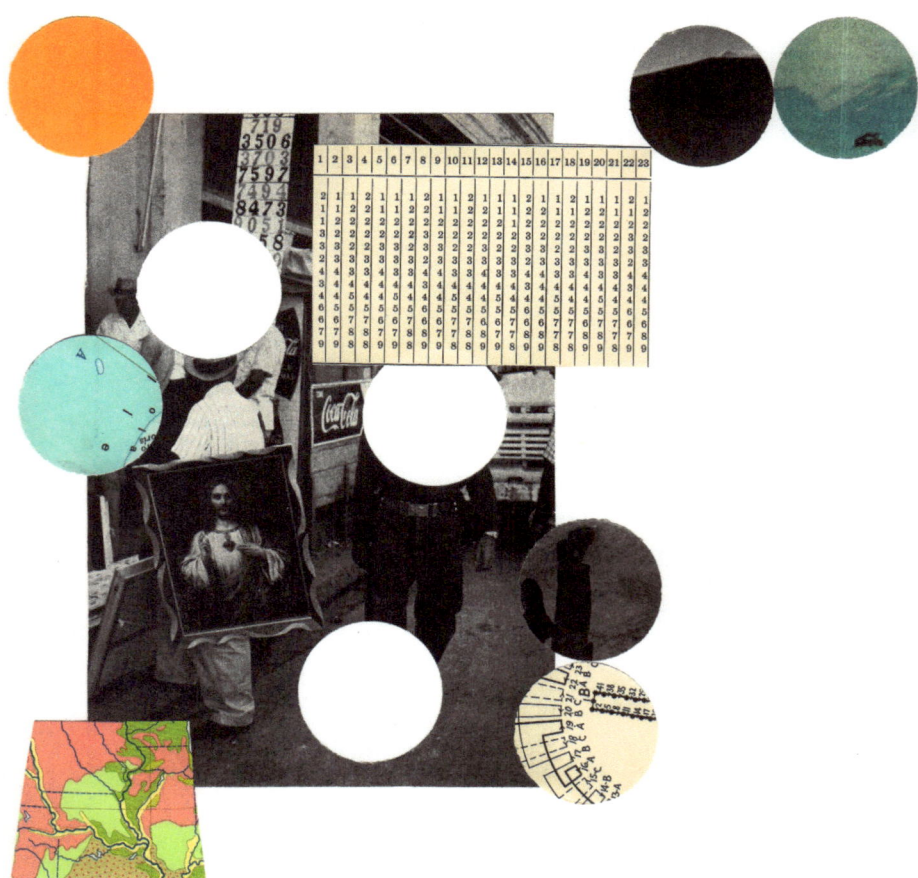

It is incredible how people can allow themselves to be bewitched by words.

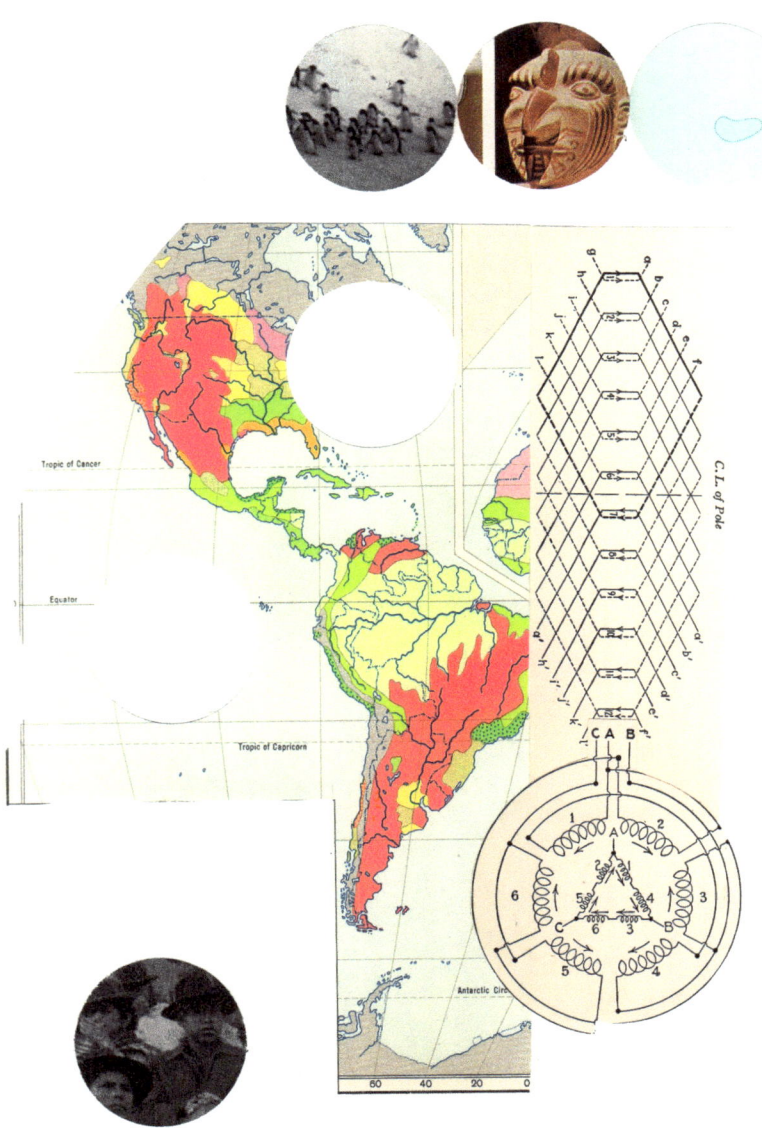

Space and time are simply *there* – an arena in which the world plays out its endless drama – permanent, dependable and immutable.

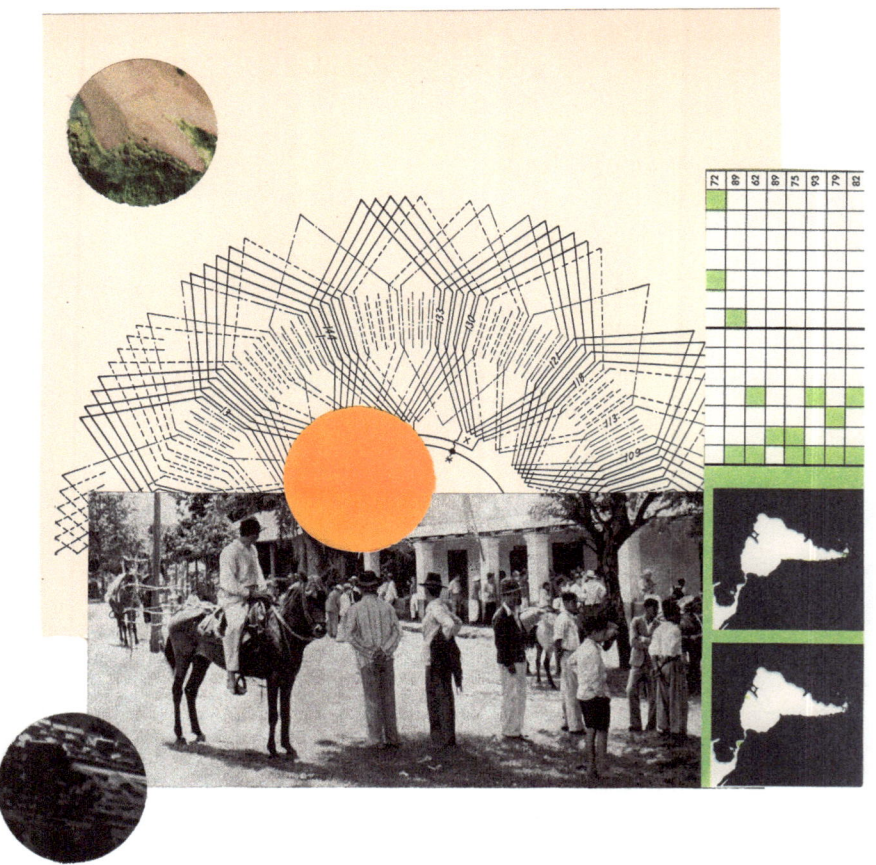

All that will be ours if we can meet the challenge of the singularity.

BOATMAN'S RETURN.

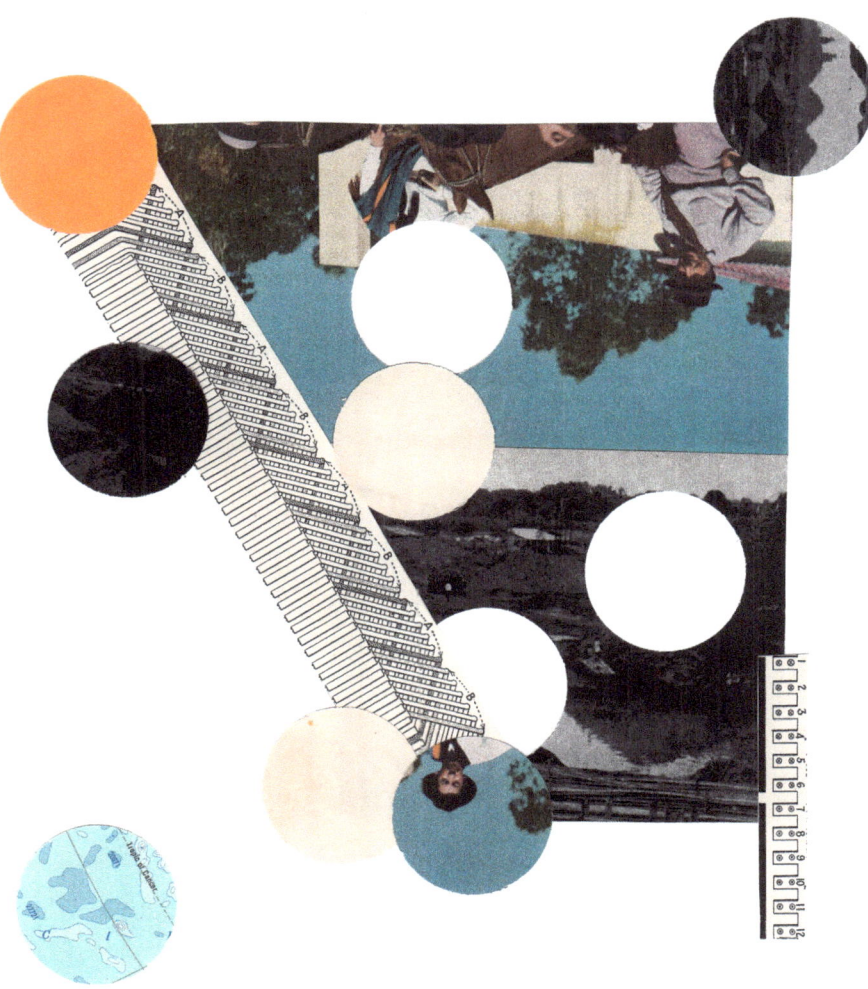

On the northern horizon a new light appeared, a small bluish gleam on the edge waters. These two lights were the furniture of the world. Otherwise there was nothing but waves.

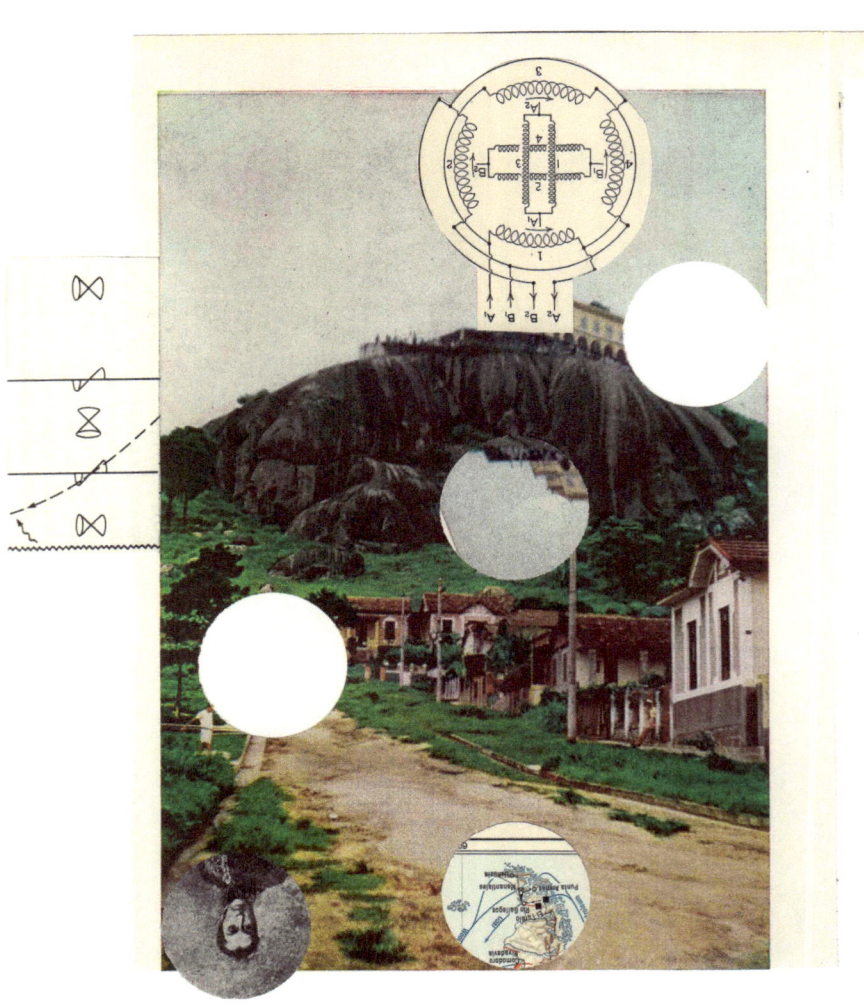

God knows where, far away on the edge of the world, he could see the glow of a brazier by a watchman's hut.

HOMEWARD BOUND.

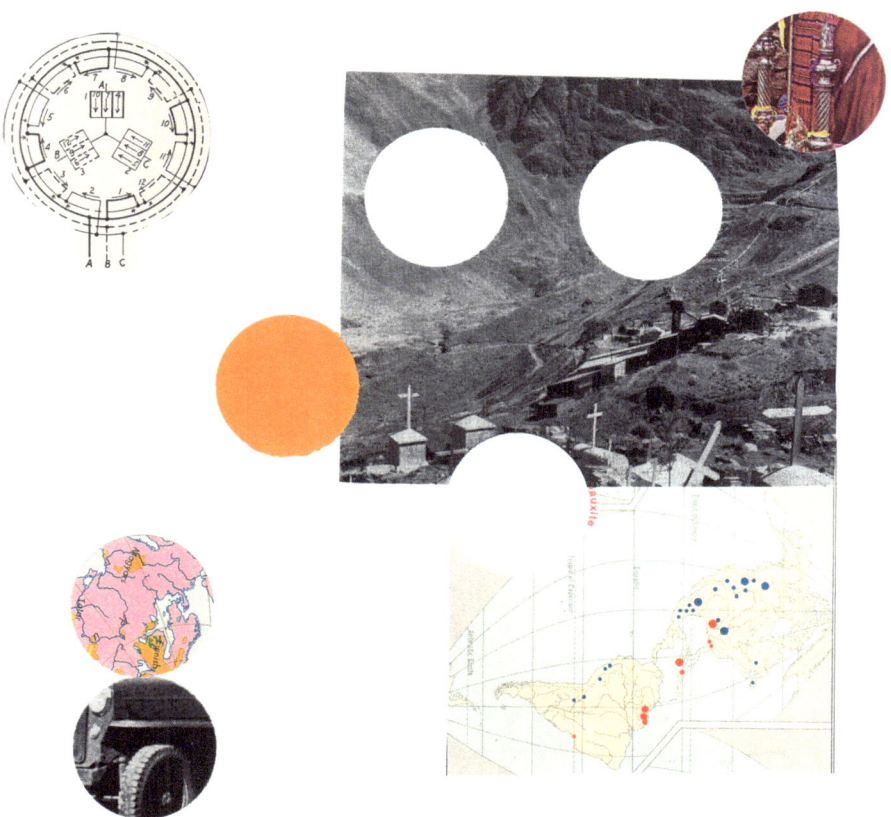

But this undertaking is arduous, and a certain indolence insensibly leads me back to my ordinary course of life; and just as the captive, who, perchance, was enjoying in his dreams an imaginary liberty, when he begins to suspect that it is but a vision, dreads awakening, and conspires with the agreeable illusions that the deception may be prolonged

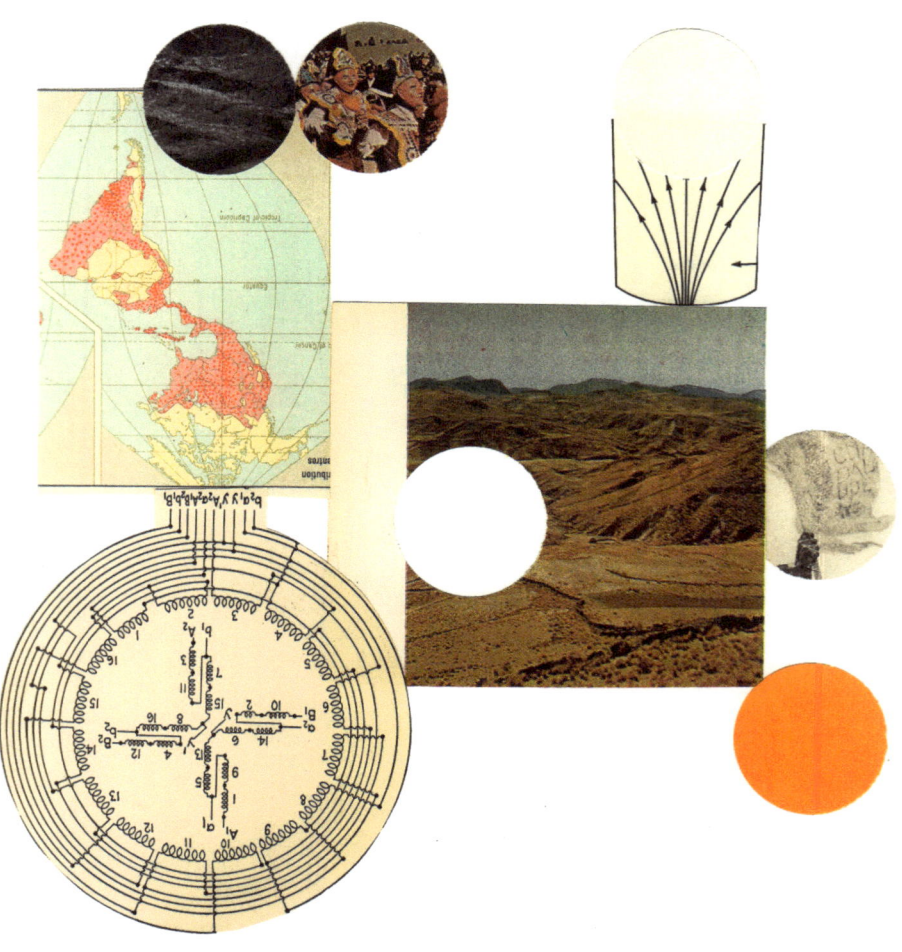

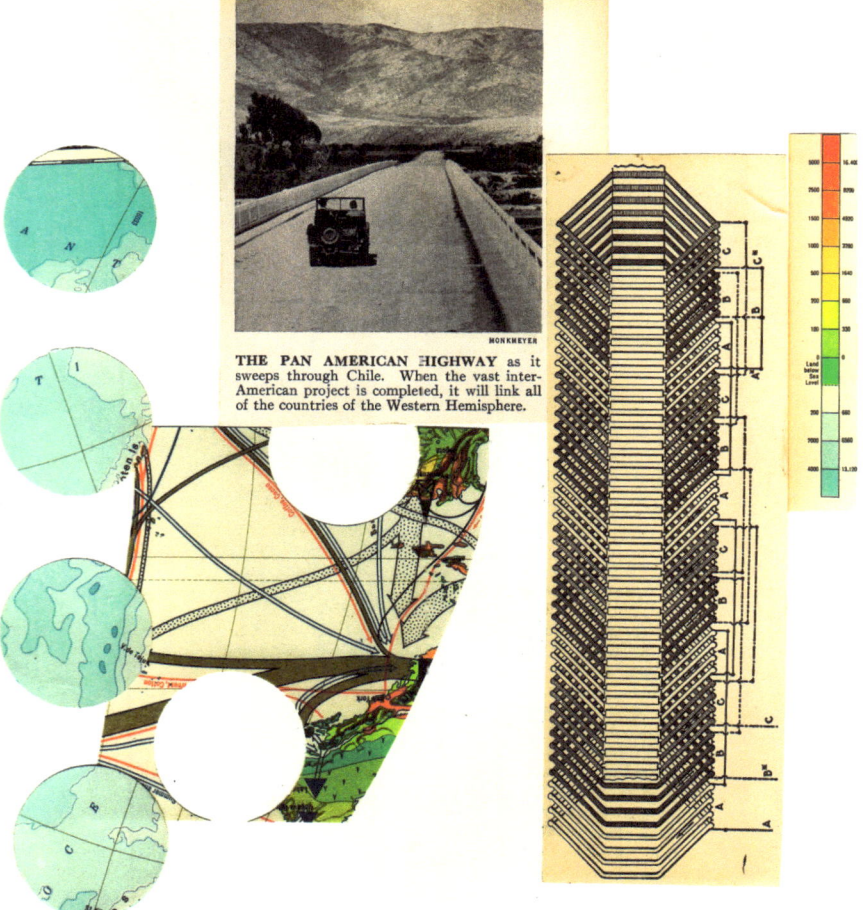

The cosmic connection

THE PAN AMERICAN HIGHWAY as it sweeps through Chile. When the vast inter-American project is completed, it will link all of the countries of the Western Hemisphere.

6 The seven bridges of Königsberg. Is it possible to cross each bridge in turn in one unbroken path without recrossing? This classic problem of topology was solved by Euler in the eighteenth century – it is impossible.

THE LAND WITHOUT A NAME

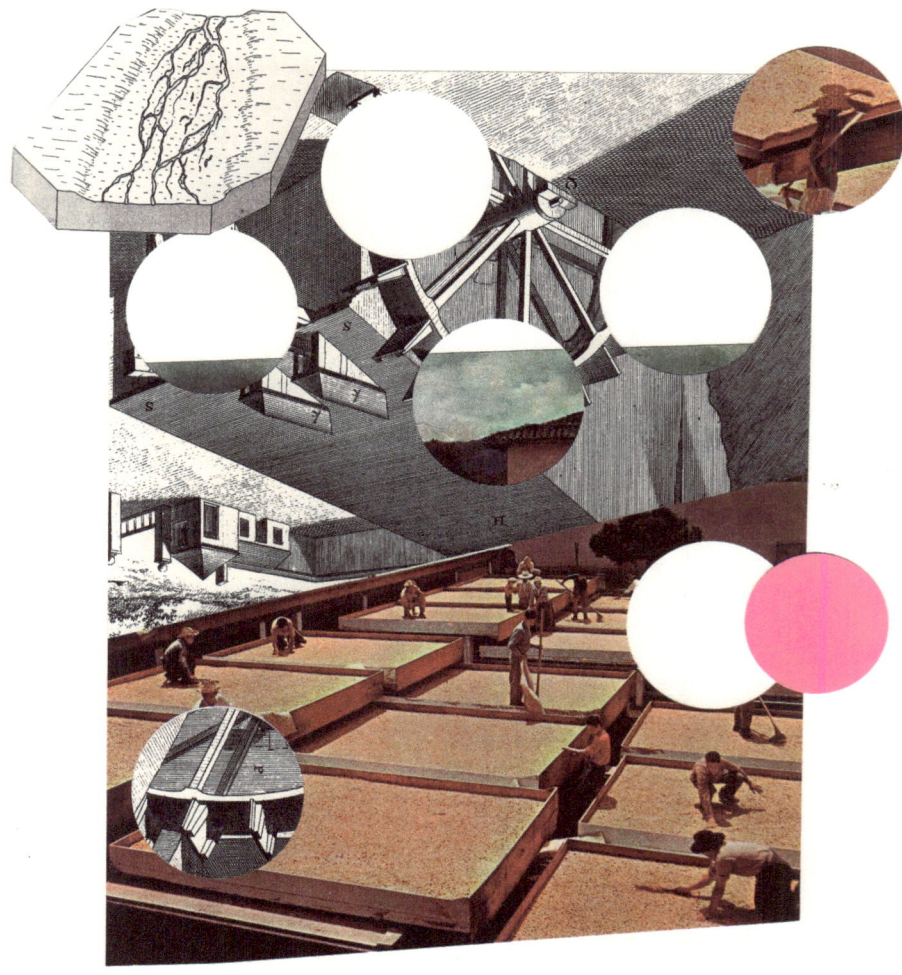

So far have we come. How far shall we go—and how rapidly?

The naked singularity exposed

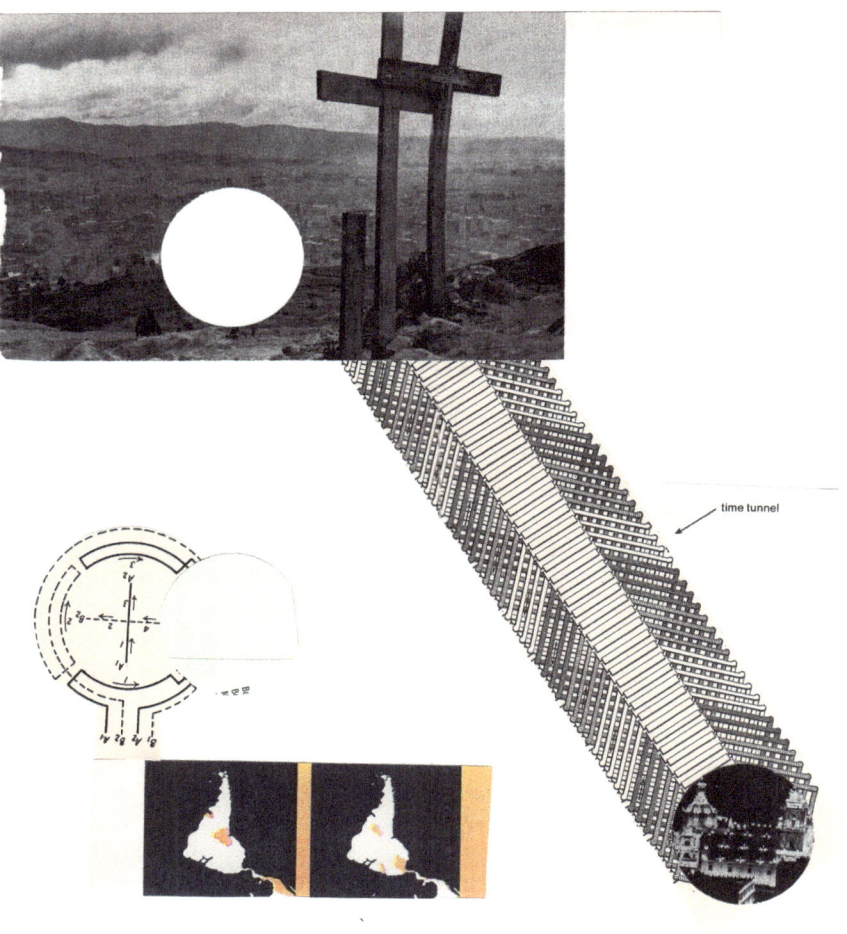

Soon there stretched out before him those deserted streets which, even in the daytime, are not so gay, and, now that it was night, looked even more desolate.

THE MEETING OF THE WATERS

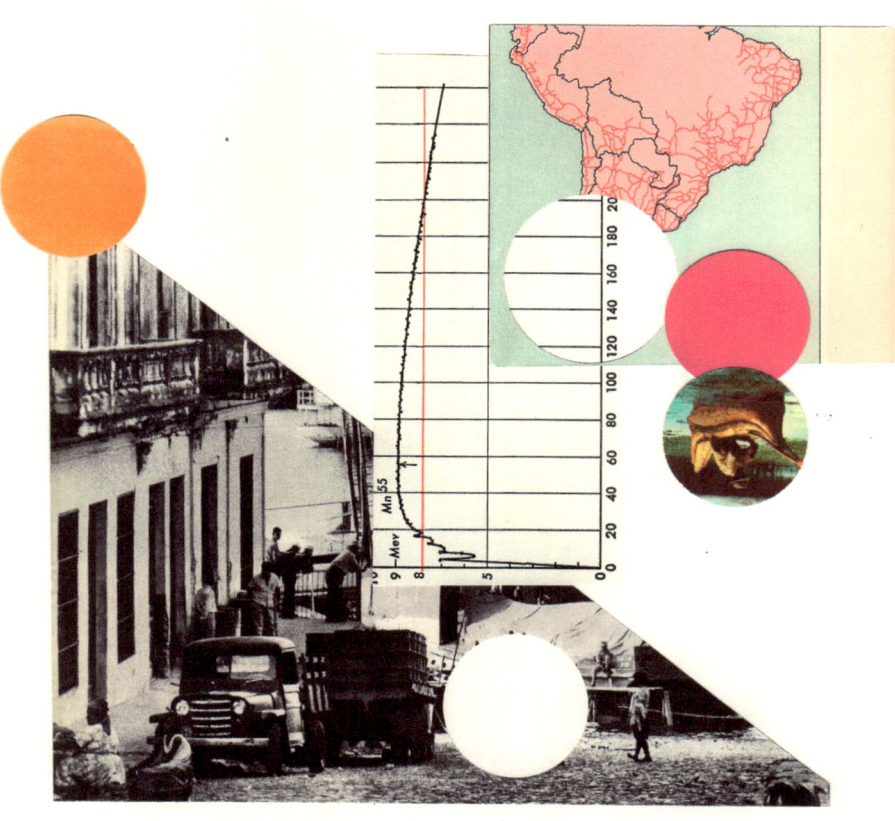

They differ as to why they believe this, but they all hold to the belief.

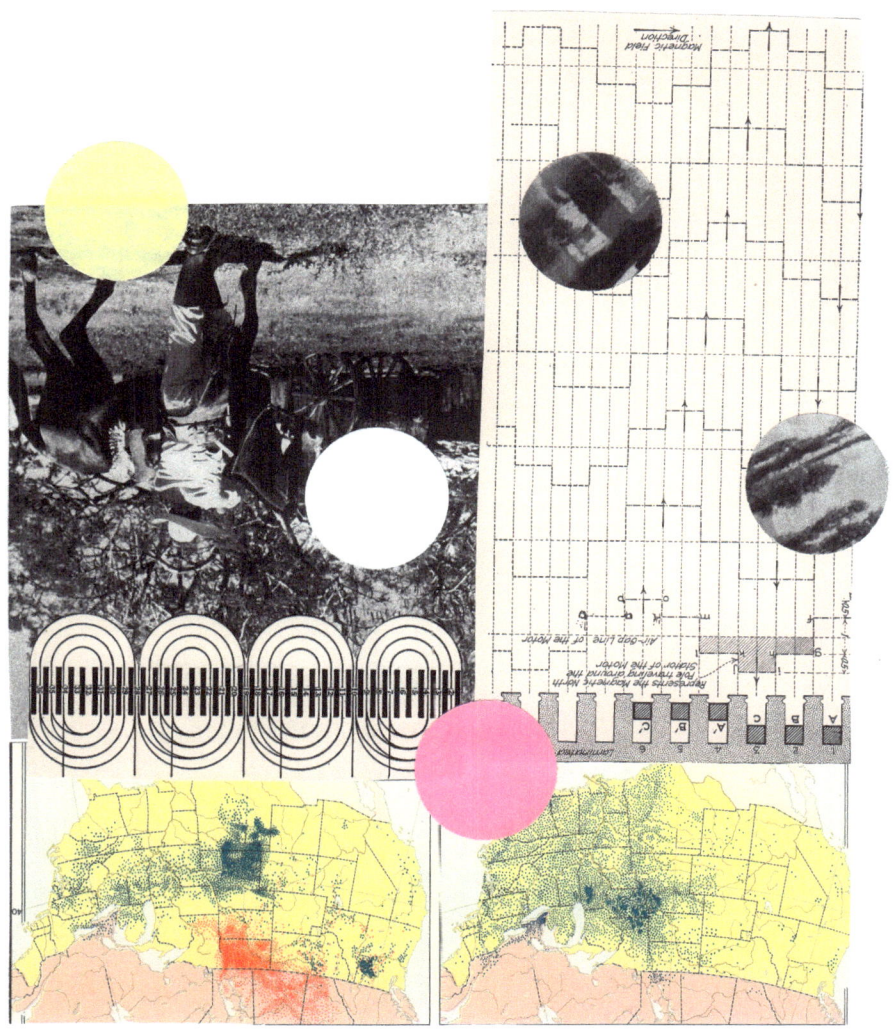

What, then, of the future?

About the Author

Pablo Helguera (born in Mexico City, 1971) is a visual and performance artist. Past art projects have included a phonographic archive of dying languages, a memory theater, fourteen visual artist "heteronyms," and four fictional opera composers. Helguera is the author several books, including *The Pablo Helguera Manual of Contemporary Art Style* (2005, English version 2007), *The Witches of Tepoztlán (and Other Unpublished Operas)* (2007), the novel *The Boy Inside the Letter* (2008), *Artoons* (Vol. 1 and 2 2009; Vol. 3, 2010), the play *The Juvenal Players* (2009), the anthology of performance texts *Theatrum Anatomicum (and other Performance Lectures)* (2009), *What in the World: A Museums Subjective Biography* (2010) and *Urÿonstelaii* (2010). In 2008 he received a Guggenheim Fellowship. In 2006 he drove from Anchorage to Tierra del Fuego with a collapsible schoolhouse, organizing discussions, activist happenings, and civic ceremonies along the way (*The School of Panamerican Unrest*). Helguera is Director of Adult and Academic Programs in the Department of Education at the Museum of Modern Art, New York. He lives in Brooklyn along with his wife, Dannielle Tegeder, their daughter, Estela, and their cat, Ceniza.

www.ingramcontent.com/pod-product-compliance
Lightning Source LLC
Chambersburg PA
CBHW040254220526
45473CB00001B/483